Burnt Sugar

Artist Avery

---

a collection of poetry and thoughts for
those with broken hearts and lost souls

Self-Published

www.lulu.com
www.twitter.com/tinylemon

ISBN: 978-1-387-58686-8

Was I Sweet Enough?

Part One

the worst part of it all
was that i could see the towers
falling down, crashing right in front of me
but i couldn't move no matter how hard
i pushed myself to get out of the way
and you watched my feet suction to the ground
and you let go of my hand and began to walk away
and i looked at you but the scream wouldn't leave my
mouth until i saw you grab her hand and pull her out of
harm's way instead
and i still didn't run, i had no effort
my knees blew out from the shaking
and my eyes closed in defeat to the debris
and i was crushed

one of the first things about you:
charles
blue fires
and unicorns
at 2 am
we are
magical

you are human,
you are impulsive,
you explore,
and you try things.

that's what i said to myself
just to excuse your actions

but why excuse
you texting her
"i love you"
every single morning

and then i would cry

and you were human
you wanted so many chances
and you told me
you would never hurt me again

and i stayed but
i should've ran
because i'm human
and my flight instead of fight
should've kicked in.

i scrubbed my body ten times
which still did not amount to how
many times i told you no
even a sugar scrub
couldn't wash away the bitter
that touched my skin those nights
i scrubbed my body ten times
until my skin itself was raw sugar
because i blamed myself for not
enforcing my no enough

was the repulsive taste of drugs
swimming to your blood stream,
that euphoria cocaine gives,

was it better than the euphoria
you described as me?

fingers sunken into my skin
like a shovel into the dirt

you told me you liked to garden once
so i figured you were planting something

but your fingers were deep inside my chest
digging into the roots of me

curled around the very essence of my being

and instead of planting your love
you ripped my beating heart from my chest

and you watched me bleed
as my body fell to the ground
planted on the soil
blood watering the earth

maybe we don't connect
like the dots i drew lines between
in my imagination

i don't understand why we can't
solve this crossword puzzle
when the solutions are on the bottom

and maybe when we color
outside the lines it's not as
pretty a picture i thought it'd be

but i was happy at moments
but my hearts in my stomach
and this is a riddle i can't solve

cause my brain hurts too much
and i'm tired of coloring books
and pixie dust

i'm tired of immaturity and games.

Artist Avery

sometimes i wonder if i was the one extra
teaspoon of sugar for your tea
that would satisfy you

but you told me you prefer honey

broken hearts and shattered lungs
i can't breathe when i'm in your arms

but that's the only place i feel safe
even when it feels like you're killing me

my broken heart in your hand and
you squeeze the pieces tighter
when i reach to grab them

let me out of your safety
so i can go be happy

i wrote a love poem once
and somebody asked me
who the subject of it was
i sort of rolled my eyes
because i was just writing
about how love should
feel in general
but when people see
our hands jumbled together
and our chuckie cheese pictures
they just know that
we are in love
so my love poems
tragedy or heavenly
the subject morphs
into this version of you
that others tend to see
they see the flowers
you've bought for me
and heard the playlist
you carefully picked for me
they see this perfect
image of our love
that we put out for them

...

...
we set up a playhouse
of a relationship
with flower lined window sills
and funny garden gnomes
with dolls of us inside
cooking each other meals
and watching endless
television while holding hands
our doll faces plastered
with the biggest smiles
we set it up in front of
a grave of a relationship
with no flowers or cards
lining the headstone our
names were etched in long ago
our cold bodies 6 feet under
wishing we were those dolls
instead of spending an eternity
with tears and arguing
with break ups and insecurities
with each other but not really
i write love poems so heavenly
that they mistake our
playhouse for reality
and ask if they're about you

love no longer lived in your eyes when you looked at me
and

you told me you didn't know when it would come back
from vacation

but just like in one of my favorite movies
vacation is just a sugar coated story of death
or pure abandonment.

i've always thought god controlled the weather but why
would he send winter just to throw summer right in the
middle of it; it's hard to decide if i'm okay with going back
to the cold again or if i want to extend my vacation in the
summer months to forever

these natural disasters are scratching my brain like hail has
destroyed my windshield and i can't see clearly anymore. i
create the tsunamis though, pushing the oceans to flood my
cheeks and stain my sleeves

earthquakes on the surface of my skin
as my heart and mind crash together like tectonic plates

i'm shivering, waiting for this cold front to be pushed out
by a warm wind but what if the warmth causes a tornado.
i'm tired of storms when i could be sheltered in his arms
already

god, if you control the weather why would you put the
sunny skies in the distance but let the snow bury my feet so
i couldn't reach them

sometimes i dreamed that another lover
would come to rescue me

the same way i'd been rescued from every heart break i
ever endured

except the one time where, i,
the damsel in distress went on an adventure

and found my prince who was not
only charming but honest
to everything he said he was being

only problem is distress doesn't fall away
the same way my rugged heart fell
and was lifted up like treasure

and i stumbled back into the woods in dismay
and fell into your grasp

tell me, why did you even catch me?

getting close to you was one of the most
perplexing things i ever went through

when your hands would graze me
my body would pull into yours

but my mind saw my body as prey
and your hands as predators

because of who i was with before you
but one day your touch became safety

and we made what i thought was love

i will never stop loving you
even if your love is the sky
and my love is the ocean below
i will never stop loving you

your love continuously changing
from bright blue to midnight black
you'll move on the same way the sky
continues on as the day dims
and then approaches again

while my love will always be flowing
for you like the ocean pushes waves
continuously and maybe some days or even some years
there will be a calm in my love
no tsunamis of missing you or hurricanes
trying to pull you back into my arms
but my love will always be there

and one day the sky will blacken and never come back and
those clouds that remind your sky that your love was once
for me won't be there. and you won't love me anymore and
my waters, my love, will be shrouded in a darkness from
you.

and it was and i still do love you

i scrubbed my body raw again
skin red after a blackened night

what was i thinking
i wasn't thinking

but i thought enough to say no
15 times

and then i told you
because even though
i gave dissent to his desire

i woke up with less clothes
than i had on when my body froze up and
i no longer had the strength to speak
all i could do was lay

and pray to god
to forgive this sin

i told you about my drunken
night blacked out in a college dorm room

and you told your buddies over xbox live
and you let them call me a liar

and then you told your friend out of anger one night that
maybe i should just go back to him
and do whatever it was that i did for him

yet the truth still is i never even gave consent for it

and now i scrub my body 10 times again

"my love is starting to go adrift,
consigned to oblivion from my heart"

my fake explanation for becoming so distant

real explanation:
"my oblivion of the poison that seeped from your love
began to disappear, so i drifted away."

chance # 999:

you hurt me again

we came to a conclusion that we should break up.
you told me you thought i'd be happier without you.

i told you that i still wanted to try but then again in
september you told me you'd probably never change.

and then when i did try to stay you told me why you really
wanted to leave and why you wouldn't do better.

you told me that i hurt you early in our relationship but you
waited until the end to confront it.

and had you told me that earlier, our story probably
would've ventured another way.

but you hadn't and i'm sorry for hurting you but my heart
ache and pain is still the same

so in summary:
i'll reminiscence on one of the last things about you.

one of the last things about you:

you liked taking pictures
of beautiful things
and i like taking pictures
of you

but you turned out to be ugly
with your hand plunged into my chest
ripping out the most beautiful thing about me
my ability to love unconditionally

<u>Searching the Cupboard</u>
Part 2

please, stop blaming yourself

i have to say almost every day

my mother always told me to come to her
if somebody touched me the wrong way.

my mother always told me to come to her
if someone broke my heart.

my mother always told me to come to her
if i needed a mother's comforting.

but i always came to myself with hate
and self-blame and some shame

and now i'm stuck with my own comfort
but it's hard to comfort myself
when i've bestowed so much
hate into myself against myself.

you were the sour marmalade and bitter kool-aid i had as a child so i kept you. i was used to the taste you brought into my life, i grew up with it.

but in order to grow i need to be comfortable with change

so now i drink tea and use only butter on my toast

i've finally bought myself some new shoes

this is significant because the last time i bought footwear
was when i bought you the slides you wanted

i searched my cupboards
throwing out any plate that a crack ran through
shattering any mugs that had been chipped
and cleaning the dust out of the bowls

I stocked the cabinets again
with sugar
with honey
with tea
and coffee

i did my spring cleaning and shopping
in the dead of winter
so when i opened my cupboards
all i would have was
unsoiled
sweetness
and the comfort of warmth

but some days still taste bittersweet so

i hope that you can't get yourself to open the saved game of
minecraft that we never finished
and i hope that you love the next person better than you
could have ever loved me.
and i hope one day i'll admit to myself that i wasn't the
problem, you just chose the fact that i was before ever
confessing it to me.
but i was there when the decision to tell me first needed to
be made just like we had to decide
whether or not to fight the monsters at night in minecraft.

and some nights stain my taste buds in disgust but

i know that
one day i'll forget about bowling together
with shy smirks on our face
cause it was our first time being a couple
when we weren't even a couple yet
and one day i'll forget about the walks we took that you
hated because you wanted to stay inside for god knows
what reasons
and one day i'll forget the way your fingers spoke poetry
when intertwined with mine cause every second of it was
worthy of a snap to a poem line
lastly one day i'll remember that you hurt me so much and
it was a good thing that you resented me and left hastily.

it's not so much that a boy ruined me
or a relationship took its toll on me

its that there was already a pain in my soul
from my diagnosis of depression
and with the heartache a process began to break down what
love i had left for myself

and i didn't stop it

and i could've stopped it

i could have left

i should have left

i've heard that with kool-aid

too much sugar in the family pitcher is self-destruction.

do you know what it feels like to destroy yourself?

not with razors against your skin. not with over sweetening
the kool-aid or lighters held too long too close to the flesh.
and no, not ignoring your hunger or giving into your
hunger too much. not looking into the mirror and
convincing yourself you aren't beautiful enough. tell me,
do you know what it feels like to destroy yourself?

do you know what it feels like to lay still, sobbing, while
your intimacy is taken by your so-called lover saying, "you
like it like that, huh?"? but you're destroying yourself
because you don't. that's why you're crying. do you know
what it feels like to convince yourself you should have
done more than say no?

it feels like destruction. your walls come crumbling down
and "no" no longer provides the protection it once did
against unwanted actions. destroying yourself feels like
scrubbing your skin raw in the shower and still blaming
yourself for their touch even though you didn't grant it.

sometimes i still pace back and forth in the kitchen
other times i scrub the dishes.

sometimes i cook a nice homemade meal to show my
depression that i have the will to keep myself not only
alive, but healthy.

a crack in the sky on a cloudy night,
i can see you in it, a lonely star sitting
right at the start, the clouds rippling around you.

you caused the split in them.
you part seas in the sky, darling
and i stare at you in admiration
falling for your brightness just like
any other stargazer you've shone upon

but you got closer to me and see stars don't do that
and the closer you got, the warmer i felt
as if heat was coursing through me
and i embraced it until you weren't a falling star
that i could catch in my hands
and hold close to my heart anymore

i still couldn't see what you were,
until that last moment hit and
the fear came in waves parting
the feelings i had for you.

you were a comet hurling right for me the entire time and
you caused my destruction as i became a star sitting alone
at the end of our love with my feelings for you rippling
around me

but then i looked around and i realized i was surrounded by
billions of stars and i shouldn't be lonely.

Artist Avery

38

deafening like airplane noises
above a house on the west side of detroit

so far self love is metaphorical to that

and i lay back
and wonder if the silence will ever be filled

i lay back
and wonder if

i will ever tell myself i love her and mean it

i've been sick for about two weeks now
on and off sore throat like a fur ball scratched it
butterflies stuck in acid in my stomach
but see, that'll get better
with a little bit o' medicine and vitamin c.

but my hearts been sick for 18 years going on 19
i don't know if the pharmacy sells a cure for that
so if i don't hit you back it's because i'm sick
and i'm busy searching my cupboards for
home remedies.

i was stargazing today

in the grains of sugar and salt

that i forgot to wipe off of the counter

i found a grain

and told myself i'd name it after me

purchased it with a lift of my licked finger

and declared it the start of my constellation

i know i've been wrong
i used to blame myself for everything
but, one day someone stepped in
told me i had did nothing worth blame
and then they hurt me
took my sweetness away
and explained again
i did nothing worth blame

but let me explain
i know i can be wrong
so i'll take sugar and pain
over hurt and outward blame
any single day

so at least, i can forgive

the both of us

Finding Sugar
Part 3

she destroys me sometimes
well, more times than my
fingers can count to

so tell me how could i love her?

this was never truly about my past lovers
but about the girl who never did love me

she's a girl that i absolutely hate
and quite honestly it's because she's
the exact opposite of me

but somehow and some way i just want her
to love me

see i'm not suicidal,
my depression is

i tell her to put down the knife
that's pushing into my stomach
like my thumb pushes
into clay when i'm sculpting

and she yells at me
pleading that it's the only solution
but in reality it's the only solution
that'll permanently kill her

i wish i could kill her
but i'm not suicidal, she is,

and if i was that knife would've
went straight through my guts
like a piece of stray sheet
metal in a car crash

a car crash is how i know
that she was suicidal
and i definitely wasn't
…

...

i had seen my death right before me
like a cliche in every horror movie
glass glittered in the lining street lights
of the highway with the black
backdrop of the cold wintry night

and when my eyes opened again
i was just so happy to still be alive

so i'm not suicidal she is

and she needs to learn to love me

i no longer scrub my body ten times
at the thought of being touched
but

i do use a sugar scrub on my lips and my hands
and a honey mask for my skin
so that

i can be as sweet and soft
as i always wanted to be

i fell in love again
before i could convince
my depression to be kind to me

so some days she yells at him
and i tell him that i am so so sorry

and other days she acts like
walking out on arguments is
the best solution she could muster

and i cry because i can't lift my feet
to go be in my lover's arms
instead of making him believe i'd ever quit on us

i'm learning to live with her,
he's learning to help me live with her
in a way i never have before

by trying to compromise

some nights i'm unable to sleep well
my bed becomes a ship hit by a storm
on the open sea tossing and turning
with me on it's deck

my clock runs a marathon that's three
minutes long but how did it get
from 10pm to 1am that quick

and those dreams are so damn real
being sucked into a vortex that
twists and turns my guts until
they're wrapped around my throat

and i can't breathe even with the
winds of the storm hitting my lungs rapidly

i still can't sleep some nights

my depression tells me that nobody could ever love me, she
still argues that i'm worth nothing

but i remember the days of being little and talking about
my perfect wedding and becoming a mother and having
that happy family after getting my degree, i remember how
yes my joy faded over the years but that was because she
made me believe that i wasn't even planning on graduating
high school let alone attending the college i'm currently at
and reconnecting with that cliche love of my life again.

but i tell her that she's the new motivation of my childhood
dreams, my drive to be joyful because lately the pain she
allowed me to endure and sometimes put me through only
makes me want to be better so i've been planning for the
future lately instead of being caught up in my past.

i fold into myself when i am around you
not in a way that i'm hiding myself

but in a way that i fold down my walls
and put away my window curtains

i fold it down like my childhood doll house
because i refuse to ever play make believe
with you like i had to do with another

i fold everything i've ever used to mask
my insecurities into myself

so that you can see me completely

i like to garden
i've sown forgiveness into my bones

and i planted flowers in my heart
to bloom around my rib cage

my lungs provide the air that
my garden needs to breathe

and my eyes shine on good days
helping with the lack of sunlight

i'm planting a garden of fruits and vegetables
i'm planting a garden of spice and love
of herbs and forgiveness

i'm replanting what some people have taken
and resowing what i have given away

the pain heard echoing through the forest
when a twig or branch is snapped in half
that's the same pain echoed by the rise
and the fall of my rib cage as my breath…

as my breath speeds up like a train on tracks
echoing the agony of the scraping metal
and when the railroad gates lower, my trembles
echo the despair of the waiting drivers…

the soft hum of their motors mimic my
muffled cries under the pillows
one driver stares at a tree while they wait
and the calm of the tree echoes your soul

though the leaves crackling under heavy feet
echo the same worry flowing from your mind
and the ridged way my ribs fall up and down
echo the increasing speed of your thoughts

…

...

you take my trembles into your soft palms
that mimic the warmth of a comfy blanket
and your voice begins to echo so loud
with the greatest sound of the world

your voice echoes and mimics love
breathing a nature into me so that my
rib cage doesn't feel the aches of broken twigs
nor is my breath a scream of agony and metal

i am no longer trembling in despair against her
or crying out the softest of car motor hums
because you're mimicking of nature's greatest song echoes
through my hollow bones

your love pulls me to shore like a life raft
as i put my hand into yours accepting safety
as i invite the tranquility of nature into my soul
from the infinite sound of your mimics and echoes

repeating the words
i love you
you're okay

i've written too many poems of heartache and pain
in my 19 years of living,

but truth be told i've only fallen in love 3 times

the first time was the first time i saw you smile

the second time was when you drove 20 miles and made a
cup of frozen yogurt just so you could see me

and the third time was when i looked into the mirror and i
could finally tell myself i loved her despite the eternal
battle she'll have with her clinical depression

but i do hope to fall in love a million more times
with you and with her

so one day i can say that i've written too many poems of
healing, loving, and forgiving to not be eternally happy
despite my past and mental illness

Artist Avery

57

i can tell her to breathe
and she'll listen now

                              and she'll stop yelling
                    out pessimistic thoughts and memories

even if she only stops for a second
i can feel more of a calm in me

                              and i can love

    i can love myself a little bit more every day now.

i build towers as tall as the ones that have fallen
collapsed like my lungs have done in the past

i use brick and mortar for foundation

i build towers in abundance so that broken souls
lost like my own before, can have a place to heal

i use love and sweetness to duplicate the structures

i build towers with no rooftops to jump from
and cabinets stocked with sugar and tea

i use words to build towers for us

one of the first things about me:

i've been hurt, i've hurt myself,
i've given up things i shouldn't have,
i've allowed myself to sit in turmoil,
i've victim blamed myself,

but

i talked to somebody about my pain,
i still breathe on the bad days,
i've forgiven and have been forgave,
i've loved, and am learning to love myself

i am in a process of self healing.

i do crossword puzzles with a cup of sweetened tea next to
me so that time will pass me by quickly

i color in page after page of my sketchbook so that serenity
can wash over me with a wave

i play connect the dots with my imagination, drawing lines
to connect my healing to the love i need to give myself

i'd like to apologize to my
reflection, to my body, to my mind, to my depression

for not loving you, for blaming you, for hurting you, for
burning your sugar.

Artist Avery

Thank you for reading my story on finding self-love.
Sincerely,

Social Media Tags:

Instagram: artist.ave   for art and poetry
Instagram: hertinylemons   for the business of it all
Twitter: tinylemon_   for both + contact here

Dedicated to those who hurt me, those who helped me, to myself, to other poets, to my best friend, to my puppy for being there for me, to "my person" for joining me on my journey to love myself better, and to my readers so they can find self-love again.

P.S. -

Chemically burnt sugar creates charcoal so if your sugar ever is burned, use it to fuel a fire of passion for yourself. Otherwise, don't let your sweetness be turned hard with caramelization. Love yourself please b/c I know what it's like not to.

Artist Avery

65